Our Earth

Written by Janine Amos
Reading consultants: Christopher Collier and Alan Howe,
Bath Spa University, UK

This edition published by Parragon in 2009
Parragon
Queen Street House
4 Queen Street
Bath BA1 1HE, UK

ISBN 978-1-4075-3794-8

Printed in China

Our Earth

Bath · New York · Singapore · Hong Kong · Cologne · Delhi · Melbourne

Parents' notes

This book is part of a series of non-fiction books designed to appeal to children learning to read.

Each book has been developed with the help of educational experts.

At the end of each book is a quiz to help your child remember the information and the meanings of some of the words and sentences. There is also a glossary of difficult words relating to the subject matter in the book, and an index.

Contents

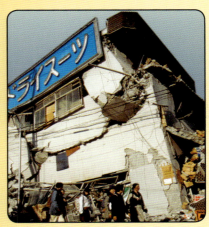

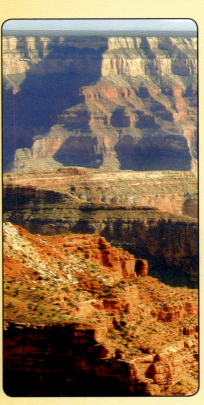

Our planet

Earth is a huge ball of water, soil, and rock. It is surrounded by air.

You cannot feel it, but Earth is always moving. In one year, it travels completely around the Sun. At the same time, it also spins like a top.

When you are going to bed, children who live on the other side of the world are just getting ready to go to school!

Earth is tilted. As it moves, places on Earth get different amounts of sunlight. This gives us the seasons.

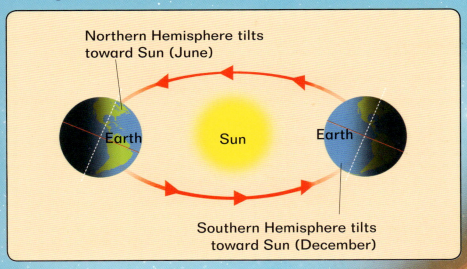

Northern Hemisphere tilts toward Sun (June)

Earth

Sun

Earth

Southern Hemisphere tilts toward Sun (December)

Earth makes one complete turn every 24 hours. It is daytime when our side of Earth faces the Sun.

A slice through Earth

Earth has layers like an onion. The outside layer is made of rock. Inside this there are rock and metal.

The thin outside layer of our Earth is called the crust. Inside this is the mantle, made of hot rock and metal. At the center lies Earth's metal core—the hottest place of all.

crust

core

mantle

Earth is wrapped in an invisible cloak of air called the atmosphere. The air we breathe in, and then breathe out, comes from the atmosphere.

The atmosphere has five different layers stacked one on top of the other.

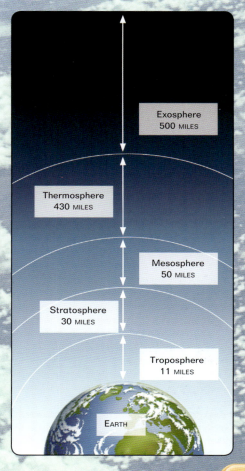

Exosphere
500 MILES

Thermosphere
430 MILES

Mesosphere
50 MILES

Stratosphere
30 MILES

Troposphere
11 MILES

EARTH

Our moving Earth

Earth's crust is cracked into massive pieces, like a huge jigsaw puzzle. These pieces are called plates. They are always on the move.

There was once one huge area of land on Earth's surface.

200 million years ago

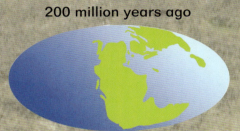

About 200 million years ago it began to split in two.

155 million years ago

About 60 million years ago the two parts broke again, and today's continents were formed.

60 million years ago

As Earth's plates move and grind past each other they can get stuck. The ground shudders—it's an earthquake!

Most earthquakes are gentle. But others can destroy buildings and harm the people inside them.

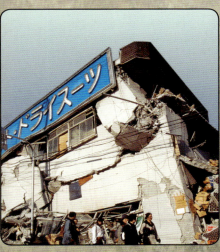

The picture below shows the crack at the point where two plates meet in Iceland.

Volcanoes

A volcano erupts when the great plates making up Earth's surface pull apart. Hot melted rock spurts out from inside.

When a volcano erupts, red-hot melted rock called magma escapes from inside Earth. As it cools it gets hard.

Volcanoes produce not just magma but also huge clouds of dust and ash.

Big, violent eruptions happen when thick magma clogs up the top of a volcano.

DiscoveryFact™

Magma that has reached the surface of Earth is called lava.

Mountains and rivers

When Earth's moving plates bump against each other, Earth's surface folds and crumples, or cracks. Mountains and valleys are made.

When Earth's plates bump and squeeze together, the crust is crumpled into mountains.

The Himalayas in Asia are the world's highest mountains.

The movement of the plates can make valleys and canyons in Earth's surface. Often rivers flow through them.

Volcanoes can also create mountains. Layers of erupted rock build up to make tall, cone-shaped mountains.

DiscoveryFact™

The Andes in South America is the longest mountain chain on land. It stretches for 4,475 miles.

Rocks and soil

Rocks cover the whole of Earth's surface. Although some rocks are very hard, they can be changed over many years.

Tree roots spread and split rocks apart. Small animals burrow and force rocks to crack.

arth   Sun   iron   tree roots   plates   frog

arthquake   canyon   volcano   lava   child

nountain   valley   rock   diamond   cave   ash

niner   coral reef   polar bear   tornado

esert   rainforest   flooding   penguins   zebra

sh   meerkats   starfish   lightning

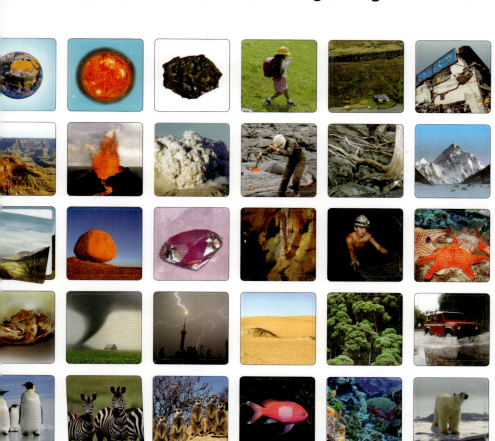

Rainwater mixed with acid from the soil soaks into the ground. It can wear away rock to make underground caves.

Metals, such as silver and gold, and rare stones, such as diamonds, are found in some kinds of rocks.

Miners dig into Earth to find minerals, precious metals, and rare stones.

Hot and cold places

Earth gets its heat and light from the Sun. The Sun's heat is strongest around the middle of Earth. At the top and bottom of Earth, the Sun's rays spread out and it is cold there.

The equator is an imaginary line around the widest part of Earth. Places near the equator are hot.

Equator

Mount Kilimanjaro in Africa is so high that it always has snow on top—even though it is close to the equator.

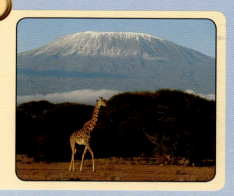

Places near the equator that are hot and dry are called deserts. It is hard for trees to grow here.

Hot, wet places near the equator are often covered with forests.

The North and South Poles are icy cold. In some places the ground is covered in snow all year round.

Stormy weather

Storms, floods, long dry spells, or very strong winds can sometimes make Earth a dangerous place.

A tornado is a tall, thin tube of spinning wind. It stretches from the clouds to the ground. A tornado travels quickly, sucking up almost everything in its path.

Tornadoes sometimes suck up frogs and fish—and drop them in a different place.

Lightning is a bolt of electricity moving from one cloud to another, or from a cloud to the ground. The lightning heats the air around it, making a loud bang. This is called thunder!

Floods happen after heavy rainfall. Streams and rivers overflow their banks. Water rushes through towns, over roads, and across farmland.

Habitats

The world's plants and animals are well suited to the places in which they live. Their natural homes are called habitats.

Coral reefs are found in tropical oceans. The coral animals feed on tiny shellfish. Reefs are also home to brightly colored fish, jellyfish, and starfish.

Penguins live at the cold South Pole. They have a thick layer of fat under their skin to help keep them warm.

Earth's big region of tropical grassland is called the savanna. Grass eaters, such as zebra and antelope, live there.

Many desert animals, such as the meerkat, have long claws for digging. They shelter underground from the hot sun.

The hot, wet rain forests near the equator have a lot of trees and vines. Most rain-forest animals live and find food in the trees.

Looking after our world

People everywhere are changing Earth. Natural habitats are in danger of being lost or ruined forever.

If you destroy an animal's habitat, the animal will die. A lot of plants and animals, such as polar bears, are in danger of dying out forever.

Most of the world's energy comes from fossil fuels, such as coal, oil, and natural gas. These fuels can make the air dirty—and supplies are running out.

People are figuring out ways to get cleaner energy from the wind, the Sun, and the waves.

Our waste is buried in huge landfill sites, which can damage the land.

You can reduce waste. Reuse glass bottles and jars, and recycle paper, plastic, and metal.

Quiz

Now try this quiz!
All the answers can be found in this book.

What is Earth surrounded by?

(a) Air
(b) Dust
(c) Sugar

Which is the hottest place inside Earth?

(a) The mantle
(b) The crust
(c) The core

Magma that has reached the surface of Earth is called what?

(a) Sand
(b) Lava
(c) Granite

Which are the world's highest mountains?

(a) The Andes
(b) The Rockies
(c) The Himalayas

What is lightning made of?

(a) Electricity
(b) Paper
(c) Metal

Where are coral reefs found?

(a) In rain forests
(b) In tropical oceans
(c) In New York

Glossary

Atmosphere   The invisible cloak of air that surrounds Earth. It is made up of gas, water, and dust.

Continent   A large area of land. Continents are often surrounded by oceans.

Equator   An imaginary line that runs around Earth, halfway between the North Pole and the South Pole.

Fossil fuel   A fuel that has been made from the remains of plants or animals. Coal, oil, or natural gas are fossil fuels.

Habitat   The natural home of a plant or animal.

Mineral   A chemical substance that can be found in Earth's crust. Minerals are the building blocks of rocks.

Plates   The huge pieces of rock that make up Earth's surface.

Planet   A large ball of rock or gas that travels around a star.

Poles   The areas at the very top and bottom of Earth.

Index

Acknowledgments

t=top, c=center, b=bottom, r=right, l=left

Artwork supplied through the Art Agency by artists including
Peter Bull and Myke Taylor

1 Digital Vision, 3 Digital Vision, 4 Oleg Fedorenko/Dreamstime.com, 5tl Gary Braasch/Corbis, 5br, 6 Digital Vision, 7 Doable/amanaimages/ Corbis, 9tr Visuals Unlimited/Corbis, 9lc Millan/Dreamstme.com 11r Mark Downey / Lucid Images/Corbis, 11l Michael S. Yamashita/Corbis, 12-13 Jim Sugar/Corbis, 13tl Gary Braasch/Corbis, 13br Roger Messmeyer/ Corbis, 14-15 Galen Rowell/Corbis, 15tr Rey Rojo/iStockphoto, 15 mr RollingEarth/iStockphoto, 16-17 Herbert Spichtinger/zefa/Corbis, 16b Joel W. Rogers/Corbis, 17tl Gerald Favre/Corbis, 17tr Oleg Fedorenko/ Dreamstime.com, 17b Ann Johansson/Corbis, 18b Layne Kennedy/Corbis, 18t Digital Vision, 19tr Digital Vision, 19br Dennis Sabo/Dreamstime, 20-21 Aaron Horowitz/Corbis, 21tr Alle/Dreamstime, 21mr Reuters/ Corbis, 21bl Tacrafts/Dreamstime, 22 Gray Hardel/Corbis, 23tl Paul Souders/Corbis, 23tr DLILLC/Corbis, 23bl Nigel J. Dennis; Gallo Images/ Corbis, 23br Tom Brakefield/Corbis, 24t Jan Will/iStockphoto, 24b Wayne Lawler; Ecoscene/Corbis, 25cr (lower) DLILLC/Corbis, 25br Rtimages/ Dreamstime, 29 Digital Vision

Additional images used on sticker sheet: second row, first picture: David Lloyd/Dreamstime.com